God's Hurting People

Pastor Vendrix Headley

Written Words Publishing LLC
14189 E Dickinson Drive, Unit F
Aurora, Colorado 80014
www.writtenwordspublishing.com

God's Hurting People © 2023 by Vendrix Headley
Revised Edition

Published by Written Word Publishing LLC 2/1/23

ISBN: 979-8-9873088-1-3 (paperback)
ISBN: 979-8-9873088-2-0 (eBook)

Library of Congress Control Number: 2023901134

Manufactured and printed in the United States of America

Dedication

This book is dedicated to God the Father, God the Son, and God the Holy Spirit. I send it forth as an encouragement to all God's hurting people who have experienced pain and anguish in different ways. Consequentially, they have unique stories to tell of the struggles and difficulties encountered along life's pathway. There is no temptation common among men for which our omniscient and omnipotent God has not provided a means of deliverance. There is simply nothing new under the sun, so our blessed Lord will never be caught by surprise at any of our adversities.

As you read this book, may you be enlightened, encouraged, and inspired by its contents. Let your mind be renewed through the power of the Holy Spirit as He transforms you into the likeness of Christ. Wallow in the assurance that you are never alone, despite the many times you might experience loneliness on your life's journey. Jesus is with you all the way and your personal victory is guaranteed in Him. Since Jesus has prayed for you guaranteeing your victory, you have no reason to fear. You can endure trying circumstances and overcome them by His grace and blood that securely covers you. Be brave and strong in the Lord, knowing evil cannot overcome you. Be excited about the crown of life that awaits you.

Table of Contents

Give the enemy
the opposite of
what he is
expecting of you.

Acknowledgments

My complete indebtedness is to my almighty Father who commissioned and empowered me to write this book to comfort His hurting people. On another level, I happily express gratitude to my husband, Venis, and my two sons, Aniel and Nashon, who stood by my side during this divine assignment. Deep gratitude is also due to a beautiful and precious pearl, my mom, Daphne Butler, who prayed for me through the challenges of this book and who has been a formidable powerhouse of influence on my spiritual development.

I am also thankful to several other people for a variety of reasons. Thanks to Pastor Keisha for proofreading my first draft, Kathy Culla and Apostle Barbara Connell for their contribution in editing and suggestions, Written Words Publishing LLC for their specialized work and final touch, and Pastor Garfield Danclar, Dr. Albert Alford, Dr. Pauline Walley, and Reverend Cephas Agabisi for being presenters at the "God's Hurting People Conference." Thanks also to Pastor Joe Samuel, who could not attend the conference because of sickness but shared his helpful insights. Thanks to the supporters and contributors to the first conference, particularly Nichole Gordon, who crossed borders to attend.

I am mindful of Merel Sterling, my aunt, who was a special influence on my early upbringing. With a sense of delight, I make mention of Pastors Sterling, Beckford, Smith, Campbell, and Taylor, who have been sources of encouragement and other forms of assistance. Finally, I would also like to thank Dian Moodie, Monica Walters, Millicent Smith, Devon Creighteny, and a host of other caring people, names too numerous to mention, for a variety of different kinds of support and influences, all of which contributed to bringing me to the completion of this book.

Reminders from Sacred Scripture

"...Count it all joy when you fall into various trials," (James 1:2 NKJV).

"For I reckon that the sufferings of this present time are not worthy to be compared with the glory which shall be revealed in us" (Romans 8:18).

"...the kingdom of heaven suffers violence, and the violent take it by force" (Matthew 11:12 NKJV).

When Jesus

says yes, no one

can say no.

Introduction

After eight months in which I specifically experienced the presence of the Lord, I felt impressed that He was calling me to counsel His hurting people. Although what I experienced moved me to uncontrollable tears, I soon forgot the spiritual encounter. After a few months, the Spirit of the Lord came to me a second time, but this time in a vision where I saw myself teaching counseling in a college. The dream awakened me with a troubled spirit. I again treated the matter callously until the Lord shook me up for a third time during my personal devotions. This was a traumatizing experience of the overwhelming presence of God. It instilled the fear of God in me. I do not ever want to experience anything like that again.

In this third instance, the Lord forcefully reminded me of the urgency with which I should begin counseling His hurting people. Let me assure you that when the Lord shows up with His overwhelming presence, you don't want to be on the wrong side of God's matters or be dragging your feet on the missions He has directed you to undertake.

This third encounter was so powerful, I was breathless and could not even finish my devotions. I was struck with the sense that the Lord was communicating to me the futility of my prayers if I refuse to submit to His commands. It was as if He was saying, "Why are you praying to Me if you will not listen to what I tell you to do?"

I made haste to communicate with my elder, Rev. Dr. Joe Samuel, who encouraged me to do just what God was asking. He offered his help in finding the appropriate place where I could study the subject more.

Let me pause to ask this question: Have you ever experienced the mighty presence of God? Has He ever given you a task? When the Lord gives you an assignment to carry out, He will equip you and, as He says in the Scripture, out of your belly shall flow fountains of living water (John 7:38).

The experience I had was like a fire shut up in my bones. Having a passion to be a mentor and being mentored has become more and a priority in my life. I understand why the Lord would lead me in this direction. While I am studying Christian counseling, I am receiving counseling myself.

Many answers to questions I had about life's trials began to unfold right before my eyes.

As you read this book, you will find answers to questions you have struggled with for years. You will be strengthened and encouraged in difficult times and understand God is the answer to all your problems. Moreover, you will find comforting words to remind yourself to put your trust only in God, the One who never fails.

Also included in this book are many poems and poetic expressions I composed. I listened to God and wrote only what He instructed me to. Therefore, I am confident you will be inspired and blessed by what you read.

A Personal Request

Will you agree with me in prayer? This is a personal request. Between each chapter throughout this book, I want to come in agreement with you. Please allow me to be your journeying partner, the reason being that according to the scripture, "if two of you shall agree on earth as touching any thing that they shall ask, it shall be done for them of my Father which is in heaven" (Matthew 18:19-20).

Prayer has no distance or boundaries. It breaks all barriers, leaps and bounds. This means that you and I have entered in a faith, kindred, and kingdom covenant. I will be your prayer partner. Don't worry about how far you are across the nation or world. Let your faith become stronger. All you have to do is believe.

Thanks for accepting the request.

Hush! No Rush!

Just let me communicate that which I anticipate.

There is much more to manifest that has not yet surfaced.

Pregnant with the promise of possibilities, you might even laugh at my tranquility.

Let me indulge in that which I feel long awaits.

I can feel my baby leaping.

Oh, I cried, "Leap! Baby, leap!"

As the urges get stronger and stronger,

I can't help but push, push, push!

It's time to give birth to that which long awaits.

Even though it may hurt, you must give birth.

By Pastor Vendrix Headley

CHAPTER 1

Knowing the Facts

Life's problems can only destroy us when we are ignorant of the truth of God's Words and not in union with Him. You may ask, what is the truth and what is false. The dictionary defines the word "truth" as "in accordance with the fact or reality, rightly so, real or accurate." The word "false" is defined as "not in accordance with the truth or facts, fake, seeming but not actually, disloyal."

Knowing the truth will empower you to differentiate between falsehood and authenticity. You will become adept at filtering the lies that contaminate reality. Knowing the truth puts you in a strategic position to overcome every obstacle that is laid in the path before you by the enemy whose plans are to discourage, derail, distract, and stop you from reaching your destiny.

When you are hurting, you experience pain, discouragement, and demotivation. As a result, stagnation occurs, which can eventually lead to death. Do not abort your pregnancy because of pain. These labor pains push you into action to give birth to God's purpose in you. Don't die in the fire of adversity and tribulation. Instead, know that such fire is meant to purify you and produce pure gold. It will bring out the precious gems in you. Jesus encourages us by saying, "Take My yoke upon you and learn from Me, for I am gentle and lowly in heart, and you will find rest for your souls" (Matthew 11:29 NKJV). I declare you shall not die in the fires of purification but live to proclaim the name of the Lord.

The moment you entered this world, you embarked upon the journey of life. The truth is you were not placed here coincidentally but for a purpose. Perhaps someone is busy trying to abort your purpose and stop your destiny, but the choice will always be yours to fulfill your assignment here on the earth regardless of obstacles. Your successful journeying through this life is contingent upon your union with our Lord and Savior, Jesus Christ.

Bear in mind that you can do all things through Christ who strengthens you (Philippians 4:13). You can accomplish all things only through faith. If you have faith as small as a mustard seed, you will move mountains (Luke 17:6). Do you believe this? Remember, faith cometh by hearing and hearing by the Word of God (Romans 10:17).

Scripture says the Words of God are true, and you shall know the truth, and the truth will set you free. God's Words set you free, and whom the Son sets free is free indeed (John 8:31-36). What does this really mean? It doesn't mean you will not be tested and tried. It simply means no matter what may come your way, you already know who you are and your position.

Your position is that you are free (right) indeed; once free, always free. So, it is not the difficulties, trials, or the ills of life that define you. Knowing what defines you puts you at an advantage to win. You must know that only what God says about you should define you. Therefore, bondage, depression, pain, hurt, being despised, rejection, disrespect, deception, disappointment, abandonment, invisibility, stagnation, or death do not have any dominion over you. Do you believe this?

My friend, these are tools of the enemy, but you are not controlled by the enemy. You belong to God; therefore, you have power over the tools of Satan. You also have weapons. Use them effectively.

Remember, one of the most effective weapons is the Word of God. It is the road map to your destination. It is equipped with everything you need to overcome. Do not underestimate worship, fasting, prayer, silence, discernment of spirits, heavenly language, and wisdom (just to name a few). You must know when to take advantage of these weapons and which ones to use given the situation. Without these weapons, surely, you will be defeated. The Word of God must be the tour guide for everything you do if you want a safe journey. Don't be fooled; you must know how to use these weapons.

Let's examine one of the weapons you have: prayer. It is a very powerful tool, but if you are not equipped with the Word, you will not be effective or efficient. It is not only about saying prayers. Rather, your prayers are to be effectual and fervent, and you must be in the right standing with God (James 5:16). Jesus taught His disciples how to pray in Luke 11:2.

Two Facts Everyone Must Know

- Fact #1 – The devil is the father of all lies and he comes to steal, kill, and destroy (John 8:44 and 10:10).

- Fact # 2 – Jesus said, "I have come that they may have life, and that they may have it more abundantly" (John 10:10).

So, whose report do you believe?

Taking Your Rightful Place

First things first, if you want to be in your rightful place, you must know the truth and the truth shall make you free (John 8:32). Jesus said that He is the truth and the life and if any man believes in Him, though he may die, he shall live (John 14:6 and 11:25). When you accept Jesus Christ as your personal Lord and Savior, you are set free. You will receive new life in Christ, and He will place you in your rightful position as a son or daughter, meaning you are a child of God. You have access to everything your Father has so you must act as a privileged child and take a firm stand. Once you have accepted Him, it means you belong to Him. You are no longer wandering around, not knowing what direction to take or where you are heading.

Now that you have a clear picture of where you are going, you must know where you came from. Coming or going suggests you have embarked on a path. We often refer to this path as a journey, which we can liken to building a foundation.

A foundation is a structure on which we build. Certain materials are necessary when constructing a foundation. Every building begins at some point and ends at another. Between the starting point and the end, builders ensure the best materials are used in the construction of the building. Therefore, they are confident in the strength of the structure.

As you begin your walk with God on this Christian journey, you must use the best materials to build your personal relationship with Him. Having a personal relationship will bring about intimacy and getting close to a person creates confidence.

Confidence in God will help you overcome the dreaded arrows of life that await you. You must possess some principal materials to ensure strength, stamina, boldness, and stability. They will cushion you in your tests and trials.

How to Get through Trials

1. Know the Word of God
2. Have faith in the Word of God
3. Put the Word of God to work
4. Pray

5. Stand still and see God's salvation

These basic but powerful tools will equip you for your journey. However, from the beginning of your life to the end, you will learn through experiences that will teach you wisdom. It is expedient to seek knowledge as it gives you a better understanding of who you are and whose you are.

Knowing who you are and whose you are will elevate your confidence, thus, securing your victory. This will place you in an unyielding position despite what you see around you. But it's not what you see that matters or what it looks like. Rather, it is what you know. God already told us to fear not because He will be with us wherever we go (Isaiah 41:10).

God is with you, even though the pain and hurt you feel. He is also touched by the feelings of your infirmities. Jesus is the solution. Be confident that what the devil meant for evil, God will turn around for your good, to the glory of His name (Genesis 50:20).

What can the storm do to you when Jesus is <u>in</u> the ship? What can the darkness do to you when you have the light? What can the valley do to you? God restores your soul in the valley (Psalm 23:3). How can the grave hold your body down when

God sounds the trumpet and you burst forth to reign with Him eternally?

There is absolutely no defeat when you know where you are going, whose you are, and that you have built on Jesus Christ the Rock. How durable and long-lasting your foundation is will depend on the strength of your foundation. On what foundation have you built? Can you say like the songwriter Edward Mote, "On Christ, the solid rock, I stand; all other ground is sinking sand"?

Scripture tells the story of the wise man who built his house on the rock. The storms beat upon it, the floods dashed upon it, and troubles from every direction of life compassed it about, but none of them could move or shake its foundation. It was built on the solid rock, Jesus Christ (Luke 6:48; Matthew 7:24-25).

My dearly beloved, storms, billows, woes, and troubles are on every hand, and sometimes they are so forceful and boisterous, you cannot still them. Nevertheless, you can rest assured that if you stand on the unmovable rock, you will see the salvation of God. You will also watch all the billows, woes, and troubles pass away while you are still standing. One song says it this way, "Lord, keep me safe until the storm passes by." If you have started by building on Christ, then you would have established a firm and unshakable foundation on which to build. This will empower you for everlasting destiny and eternal life.

Let Us Pray

Dear God, I come to You today, in the Name of Yeshua (Jesus), Your Son and my Savior. Lord, help me to know and have confidence in the truth You told me in John 14:6. You are the truth and the life. Lord, please help me to identify with You now and forever. I understand that when I know You as my personal Savior, I will be free. Lord, help me to understand that as I go on life's journey, I will be faced with many challenges. Help me to draw back on Your Word to carry me through. In Psalm 34:19, You told me that I will experience many afflictions, and though they may seem like a flood of mighty rushing water, You promised to deliver me out of them all. Thank You, Lord. I pray in Jesus' Name, Amen.

CHAPTER 2

Knowledge is Power

According to Hosea 4:6 and Isaiah 5:13, one fundamental truth is God's people are destroyed for a lack of knowledge. Let me hasten to encourage you to seek knowledge as it will empower you to be an effective tool in the hands of the Lord. Without knowledge, you are useless to the Lord and if you reject knowledge, He will also reject your children and you cannot be a priest unto the Lord. The famous saying goes like this, "A man is a fool to what he doesn't know."

As we discussed, there are key components to constructing a foundation. Likewise, when building a personal relationship with God, you must also have key components. Building relationships take time, effort, honesty, commitment, and determination. Knowing God is the key to obtaining a victorious life; therefore, it is important to spend time with Him and read His

Word to get intimate with Him, so He will reveal His secrets to you.

One accomplished and rewarding achievement anyone can have is being able to fulfill the desires of those you love. However, this can only be achieved when you know what they love, their likes and dislikes, and strive to satisfy them. The same can be said about when you know God; you will strive to please Him.

Be aware of the fact that getting to know someone doesn't happen overnight. You get to understand them better by spending more time with them. But even when you know them better, there is always more to learn as you dedicate yourself to them. So it is with God, the more time you spend with Him the more you get to know Him. Let's put it this way: there are deeper depths and higher heights in Him.

Getting to know your love puts you at an advantage to please Him. How wonderful this relationship is when you receive this kind of attention in return. This kind of connection cannot be described as anything less than perfect. A relationship like this attracts love, trust, confidence, communication, and endless passion. When you have this kind of relationship with someone, there is no time for losing. You will know where to go when you need a friend.

Now that the importance of closeness has been established, you will be more confident to face life's giants.

Know Your Source

"Some trust in chariots, and some in horses: but we will remember the name of the Lord our God" (Psalm 20:7).

When you know who your source is, you will be confident that it cannot run dry. You can draw from your source because the reserves are endless and satisfaction is guaranteed.

God promises He will never leave or forsake you. Knowing He is always there beside you gives you a sense of security. You can now say like the psalmist, "I will lift up mine eyes unto the hills, from whence cometh my help. My help cometh from the Lord, which made heaven and earth" (Psalm 121:1-2).

Dearly beloved, it doesn't matter what you may be going through. God will not suffer your foot to be moved because He neither slumbers nor sleeps (Psalm 121:4). Did you know that going through trials is a blessing in disguise? Yes! What you go

17

through is for a purpose. You may not understand this now, but later, God will reveal His plan for your life and you will understand the awesome God you serve.

You will be happy to have gone through your trials. No wonder God says to count it all joy when you go through diverse temptations, for the sufferings will not be able to compare with the joy that shall be revealed (James 1:2). Sometimes, you might believe God has forgotten you when you are experiencing hard times. You ask yourself questions like, "Why me, Lord?" or "Lord, where are you?" The next time these questions come to your mind say, "Thank You, Lord, for choosing me." This shows true growth and confidence in your God.

He will not give you more than you can bear. Nothing happens to you that God doesn't know about. Remember, all things work together for good to them that love the Lord and are called according to His purpose.

Be encouraged, knowing that this troubled world is not our final home. The apostle Paul says, "If in this life only we have hope in Christ, we are of all men most miserable" (1 Corinthians 15:19). Thanks be to God, our Father, that we have abundant life through Jesus Christ, our Lord and Savior.

One lie you must identify and take authority over is that when you go through tribulations, you are bad. Do not believe this falsehood. God allows you to go through trials because He knows He can count on you. He is taking you to the next level. Ask yourself, can He really count on me? If the answer is yes, hold on a little longer. Take Him at His Word. He will carry you through. The victory is already secured for you. We are not without a witness; we have Job as a living example. Read the Book of Job. You can make it! Seek God's joy; you will find strength in it.

Let Us Pray

Heavenly Father, I pray today You would grant me knowledge. I have come to realize that the lack thereof is dangerous. God, I cannot do anything without the understanding of what I am doing. Father, Your Word declares in Hosea 4:6 that Your people are destroyed for lack of knowledge. I can see that the lack of knowledge spells disaster and destruction. Lord, now I understand what You mean in the scripture. Father, You specifically told me that You will not use me to do anything and You will even reject my children if I lack knowledge. Timothy endorsed the importance of having the knowledge to avoid embarrassment. In 2 Timothy 2:15, it is written that I must study to show myself approved. So, when I speak, I will only state fact and be confident that I am representing You correctly. Help me to consider Your Words. In Jesus' Name, I pray. Amen.

CHAPTER 3

God's Timing

God's timing is always on target. He is never late. Remember, it's neither your way nor in your time. It is in God's time. Trusting God allows you to see His glory in all things. I mean all things. All things work together for good to them who are called according to God's purpose (Romans 8:28). This scripture is repeated daily, but do you stop to understand what it means? You should answer this question but think seriously before giving your response. If your answer is yes, then you understand it. So, the next question is why do you become so discouraged, hurt, and depressed so often?

If you know He is working out His purpose in your life, then you should be in a better frame of mind. You should be in a place of rejoicing, praise, worship, hope, and the list goes on and on.

Ask yourself this question, is this possible? I will be the first to answer yes, it is. Can you have joy even amid trials? Yes, my friends. Feeling happy is not real joy. Happiness only lasts for a short time until that which makes you happy is taken away. On the other hand, joy is everlasting, and no one can take it away because joy comes from the Lord. In Him, you will find strength.

You must endure hardship. It is one mark of a good soldier. If you labor and faint not, you will receive a crown of life. God has a plan for your life. He says it's a plan of good and not of evil. He will give you an expected end.

What is your expectation of God? Think about it carefully. Expectation means to wait with great anticipation, knowing you already have what you are waiting for. Hebrew 11:1 makes it clear that faith is the substance of things hoped for, the evidence of what you have not seen.

Many can attest to having experienced the blessings of faithful friends in their lives. When they have a need, they already know, that once they ask, they are sure to receive, and are confident what the answer will be. If you have such confidence in your earthly friends, you can have much more in God.

Jesus said if earthly parents know how to give good gifts to their children, how much more will God give to those who ask Him (Matthew 7:11).

God loves you so much that He gave His only begotten Son that you may have life more abundantly (John 3:16). Wait on the Lord. He will renew your strength. He said you shall mount up with wings like eagles; you shall run and not be weary, walk and not faint (Isaiah 40:31).

If you are truly convinced, you will never doubt Him again. Waiting on God suggests total confidence and rest that He will come through for you. Job was willing to wait on God. Even though everyone around him was losing hope, Job refused to doubt God.

This is the kind of faith that will move God to work on your behalf. Job said it doesn't matter how long it takes, He will surely wait. God is looking for Job-like faith. The truth is God is not moved by your trials, your difficulties, or even when you are threatened by death. He is absolutely moved by your faith in Him, whether in life or when faced with death. If He was moved by trials, He would have stopped Daniel from being thrown into the lion's den and the three Hebrew boys from being thrown into the fiery furnace. Your unshakable faith in the most dreadful and dangerous times of your life will move God to work on your behalf. Always remember that you are not a victim; you are a victor, meaning you are victorious.

Only those whose lives are totally sold out to God can truly trust Him in moments like these. This will testify, that you love Him for who He is, and not what He can do for you. This is an extraordinary kind of faith that calls for an extraordinary kind of action. Even what looks like the end is not too late for God. He will allow you to be tested beyond measure to glorify His name. God must get the glory. Remember, you are not your own; you belong to Christ, and He will take care of His own. You may not understand the mystery of God. His understanding is past finding out because His ways are far different from your ways. You cannot live on your own expectations. You will find yourself in a tight spot when you want things done your way and in your timing. Scripture reminds you not to be anxious about anything but in prayer and supplications, make your request known to God with thanksgiving (Philippians 4:6).

You must come to grips with the fact that many times you suffer lack because of disobedience. Your life is not in accordance with what the Word of God says. If you want God to move in your life, you must make the conscious choice to walk in harmony with His Words.

God has already spoken. He has already laid down His cause and effect. He cannot go back on His Words. He said, "Do not be unequally yoked with unbelievers" (2 Corinthians 6:14). What if you choose to marry someone who does not believe in God? After you have been married for a few years and your spouse begins to act up and do some outrageous things, what will you do? Who will you ask to help you? If you say you will ask God, how will you direct your prayers to Him? What will you expect Him to do?

Bear in mind, God honors His Word higher than His name. Therefore, you must take what He says seriously. Do not twist His Words to suit your feelings and when trouble comes expect Him to act outside of His Words to help you. God is a merciful God, but He is also just. Hence, you must face the consequences of your disobedience.

Let Us Pray

Dear God, You are the God of timing. Please help me to patiently wait on You. In Isaiah 40:31, You told me that the strength of those who wait upon You shall be renewed. You promised elevation to those who wait. You promised that I will be able to run the race to the end as only those who make the finish line will be rewarded the crown of life. I will also continue the journey I have started with You. I will not grow weary nor faint. Lord, my prayer today is for You to teach me how to wait. I pray in Jesus' Name, Amen.

CHAPTER 4

Peace in the Valley

To everything, there is a time and season. And valleys are part of those seasons. The valley is not always a bad place to be. You may just have to take a retreat there. You will not be in it forever. The valley is just a part of the process; it is where the Lord restores souls. He will lead you beside still waters that represent peace. There is no greater joy than to have peace in the midst of your valley experience.

Our God is a God of everything. We are His sheep, and He is our loving Shepherd. He will not withhold any good things from us. Our God is a God of diversity. There is no mountain too high He cannot climb and no valley too deep He cannot reach. He is the God of the valley and the mountains too, so do not be afraid. Your time is coming. You are coming out.

We must all go through the valley, and when you are placed there, it is for a purpose. A valley is also a unique place. My experience in the valley may not be yours. However, we should have one thing in common: the boldness to face our valleys. The valley is one aspect of life we will not escape.

When you understand what the valley does for you, you will know when you are in it that there are lessons to be learned. Take the time in the valley to introspect and evaluate your life. Some of the choices you make can definitely lead to valley experiences.

The choices you make in your life will affect you in one way or another. However, you will not die in the valley. Psalm 23 says that though you walk through the valley of the shadow of death, you should fear no evil because the Lord is with you. His rod and staff will comfort you. So even in the valley, you can find comfort.

What an awesome assurance! What an awesome God we serve! May I share a revelation with you? Valleys are often referred to as trials, difficulties, and hardness. Mountaintop experiences are seen as living in victory and times when you are in your glory and you shine. But did you know the time on the mountain is the most dangerous time in your life? It is there that you let down your guard. When you are on top of your mountain, you must be very vigilant because you are exposed to the enemy and can be brought very low.

Remember, if you are down in the valley, you can only be lifted. When you are in the valley, the devil cannot kill you. That power was not given to him. He may touch your body but not your soul. However, on the mountaintop, if you fall suddenly, when the enemy takes you unaware, you can die. Nevertheless, your life is in God's hands. He is in control.

What is important is wherever you find yourself, you must have the Savior with you. The songwriter Fanny J. Crosby says, "I must have the Savior with me for I dare not walk alone. I must feel His presence near me and His arms around me thrown. Then my soul will fear no evil; let Him lead me where He will. I will go without a murmur and His footsteps follow still."

In the Valley

God is touched by the feelings of your infirmities.

When in the valley, way down deep below, it may seem there is no place to go.

No need to worry, for it may just be the place for you to grow.

Don't be mad or sad, only fear God.

He is the Almighty One.

Jesus cares and loves you, so He will guide your steps wherever you go.

The world will see that you surely know.

Whether in the valley or on the mountaintop, Jehovah is the God of them all.

By Pastor Vendrix Headley

Let Us Pray

Our Father which art in heaven, hallowed be thy name. Thy kingdom come, thy will be done in earth, as it is in heaven. Father, You are my source, even when I am in the valley. Lord, sometimes when I am in the valley, I tend to lose focus. Lord, please give me courage. Help me to understand that the valley is not always a bad place. Help me to remember that there is where you restore me. Help me to be still in moments like this. Give me the strength to allow You to lead me. You are planting me in a good place. You put me beside still water where I can grow, be refreshed, and be fruitful in due season. I will constantly produce precious fruit. Help me to be aware of my evergreen tree where my leaves will never wither. Hallelujah! Lord, help me to stop taking my valley for punishment. In Jesus' Name I pray, Amen.

CHAPTER 5

Don't Miss Your Destiny

Don't be fooled; the Bible says as newborn babes we must desire the milk of the Word that by it, we will grow (1 Peter 2:2). Every destiny child needs what is called leadership and mentoring to take the correct path to his destination. The Spirit of the Lord can and will guide you into all truth. Nevertheless, God puts people in place to lead. God called Moses to lead His children out of Egypt into the Promised Land. Your leaders play a very important role in your life as you prepare for your journey to your destiny.

You must be focused and vigilant because many things can prevent you from reaching your destiny. Distraction is one thing you must look out for, and it comes in various ways. You must keep your eyes on the prize. Knowing the voice of your God will help you to follow His direction. There are many voices out there to deter you from your destination. It is important to study the Word of

God, so you can show yourself approved, rightly dividing the Word of Truth. What does this mean? It means to stand only in the truth of God's unadulterated Word. To divide means to share, separate, or take apart. As it relates to God's Word, it is to comprehensively separate the truth from lies.

This can be done in words or actions. You may have to move away from environments that are not conducive to godliness. God told us in His Word to "Come out from among them and be ye separate" (2 Corinthians 6:17). In other words, take a stand on the Word of God.

Never allow anyone who is not led by the Holy Spirit of God to lead you. A person who is not led by the Spirit of God is ignorant, full of self-righteousness, and does not follow the instructions of the Word of God. This is dangerous. Run for your life! Remember, ignorance and illiteracy kill and cause unnecessary pain to you and also those around you. The contents of this book may be simple, but I implore you not to let them go. Ponder these things and, in them, you will find the truth.

Philippians 4:8 tells us, "Whatsoever things are true, whatsoever things are honest, whatsoever things are just, whatsoever things are pure, whatsoever things are lovely, whatsoever things are of good report; if there be any virtue, and if there be any praise, think on these things."

Train your mind to think on things that will edify you and those around you. Your mind plays a great role in cultivating the battlefield on which warfare takes place every day. Remember, in war, some may be wounded and some may even die. Therefore, be ready at all times to fight the good fight of faith. The weapon of our warfare is not carnal but mighty through God to the pulling down of strongholds (2 Corinthians 10:4). You must keep your weapon sharp and handy.

What are some of the weapons with which you must fight? The main one is the Word of God. All the skills, power, and protection are there for your victory in the fight. The weapon of prayer is effective, and the weapon of worship is dangerous. Sometimes, the weapon of silence can tear down a whole city and hiding for a moment will get you victory. Do not become complacent because complacency causes lethargy, lethargy brings weakness, and weakness can lead to death.

I Am a Purpose

Hi! Hello! Over here!

Beckoning night and day.

No one seems to hear the voice that cries.

Trying to convince me you are invisible.

Are you for real?

I am human.

Why don't they understand?

Why don't they look my way?

I have a vision.

I have a dream.

I have a purpose.

Can't they see?

Can't they look?

I turned away, looking up to the sky,

Questioning, "God what do they not
understand?"

I ask, "Lord, do I go, or do I stay?"

The answer comes,

"Just to be clear, it's not what you think

Or what you feel. It's what is my will.

Just be still."

Clearly, can you see what this might be?

God's will is fulfilled in me

Though evil humans may be

So let God arise in me,

His purpose they all will see.

By Pastor Vendrix Headley

Be careful of stagnation. Avoid being stuck in one position for too long, especially when there is no growth or fruitfulness. Don't even hang around certain places. You must know when your season is over. It is important to be led by the Holy Spirit and to be purpose-driven as you are placed here for a purpose.

Get Rid of Doubts!

I have been directed by the Lord to do a few things, and I am absolutely sure when the Lord speaks to me. God asked me to hold a conference called, "God's Hurting People." Wow!

Yes, I started putting things in place but as the time drew nearer, the human part of me kicked in. One day, while I was coming from one of my sons' P.T.A. meetings, I was thinking about the whole thing. Questions invaded my mind: What if no one turns up? What if? What if?

The Lord put me to shame. He asked me "Have I ever let you down?"

My answer was, "No, Lord, you have never let me down."

I smile with great confidence. That conference was a great blessing to me and all those who attended. As it was noised abroad, those who were not there started calling and have already booked for the next year. Look what the Lord has done. If God gives you a commission, He will also make the provision.

Let Us Pray

Heavenly Father, I give glory to You, the Almighty One, King of Kings, Lord of Lords. I thank You that when You created me, it was not coincidentally, but You created me with purpose. Glory, Hallelujah! I recognize from conception the devil tried to kill me. He tried in various ways, but he did not prevail. Thank You, Jesus. Lord, I am aware of the fact that the devil is a thief and he comes to kill and destroy but here You win again. You came and gave me, not just life, but abundant life. Hallelujah! God, help me fulfill Your purpose in me. Lord, I am available to You. Bring forth destiny to live in me. Let Your will be done. You will get the glory. Let there be no miscarriage. Let me give birth to purpose. In Jesus' Name, Amen.

I am aware you have read this in the beginning, but this is what's called meditation. Think about this. Sometimes, you step out to do things and you meet the naysayer. Tell them to HUSH! Hallelujah!

Hush! No Rush!

Just let me communicate that which I anticipate.

There is much more to manifest that has not yet surfaced.

Pregnant with the promise of possibilities, you might even laugh at my tranquility.

Let me indulge in that which I feel long awaits.

I can feel my baby leaping.

Oh, I cried, "Leap! Baby, leap!"

As the urges get stronger and stronger,

I can't help but push, push, push!

It's time to give birth to that which long awaits.

Even though it may hurt, you must give birth.

By Pastor Vendrix Headley

CHAPTER 6

How to Run with Your Vision

Strategize

Believe in yourself and then others will believe in you. Don't feel bad if others don't see your vision. It is your vision. A person without a vision can only see right where he is. Be careful of visionless folk.

"But without faith it is impossible to please Him,..."
(Hebrews 11:6 NKJV).

"Where there is no vision, the people perish..."
(Proverbs 29:18).

It is said that you can share in other people's visions. You do not have to be the visionary; you may just be the vehicle the Lord chose to help bring the vision to fruition. Therefore, you must beware of selfishness and learn to be a sower so you can reap when harvest time comes around.

I Have a Dream

Carefully choose those with whom you share your vision. Do not be deceived; many dream killers are out there.

I can remember sharing my vision with someone I respected and looked up to for guidance and encouragement. She said to me, "You're always doing something." This was in a negative voice. My feelings were crushed. I was very disappointed in someone I considered a spiritual friend. I had to quickly say to that person, "Whatever the Lord tells me to do, I will do."

Know your associates and those you should stay away from when God births a dream or a vision inside you. You can know them by their fruits. When you see the fruits manifesting, do not ignore them. Be as wise as a serpent and harmless as a dove (Matthew 10:16).

Avoid negative people; they can abort your dream. A healthy environment is vital to the healthy birth and growth of any vision. Giving birth to anything is good; however, it is imperative to be aware of your surroundings. When a mother is expecting the arrival of a new family member, much preparation is made to ensure a smooth birth and transition. Likewise, you must make the necessary preparation to give birth to your visions.

What is Wrong?

God intended that you prosper and be in good health, even as your soul prospers. This is God's perfect will for your life. Have you ever stopped to think about why you are not living and experiencing the fullness of God's divine will in your life? One may say it is because of disobedience or even for some other reasonable and logical reason. Any of the above can be considered, but there is one main factor: you do not indulge in the abundance of God's presence daily.

Our daily goal is to be in God's presence. There, every other activity perishes. You will begin to experience the fullness of joy as you are immersed in God's unending pleasures. This happens when you understand who God is. How can you please God if you don't know Him or His attributes? You must first know Him to please Him.

"But seek ye first the kingdom of God, and his righteousness; and all these things shall be added unto you" (Matthew 6:33).

Don't miss this important word in the preceding verse: "seek." You seek when you want to find something or if you are looking for answers. What does God say about seeking? He said He is a rewarder of those who seek Him diligently (Hebrews 11:6).

He also told us to knock, and it shall be opened; ask, and it shall be given (Matthew 7:7). It is important to understand what it means to knock, ask, and seek as you use these words in your everyday life. Let's examine the meaning of each word.

Knock

Webster's dictionary defines the word "knock" as "strike a blow to rap on a door or to make a thumping noise; that is said of an engine." Three distinguished words arrive from this meaning that suggests an intensity of force. David understood what it meant to seek; it is what drove him to pen Psalm 42:1 (NKJV), "As the deer pants for the water brooks, So pants my soul for You, O God." David was desperate to be restored and revived. The desperation was so intense, he was willing to have his situation resolved. He turned the searchlight inward and recognized the innermost part of his being was in a position of defeat. In distress, David cried out to his soul and asked why?

"Why art thou cast down, O my soul? and why art thou disquieted in me?..." (Psalm 42:5).

The answer lies within him. He knew what the solution was, and he activated it when he commanded his soul to hope in God. He said, "For I shall yet praise him for the help of his countenance" (Psalm 42:5). When you knock, you will anticipate a response as you eagerly wait.

Ask

Webster's dictionary defines the word "ask" as "to use words in seeking the answer to a question, to inquire of, to request or demand, to invite." Asking implies the curiosity of knowing, looking for answers, getting feedback to an inquisition, or making a request. Like knocking, when you ask, you also anticipate a response as you await the answer, whether favorable or unfavorable.

Seek

The word "seek" is defined by Webster's dictionary as "try to get, try to find, aim at, and search for." The word "seeking" comes from the word "seek." It is desperation to find, to achieve, to know, and to go after.

Now that you are more aware of what these words mean, you will use them in their active places.

Remember, it is important to seek knowledge, which is a powerful tool to please God and bring good success. Be aware of the fact that you will face harder times in your life if you are unlearned because the lack of knowledge leads to destruction.

Rise in the name of the Lord and begin your inquisition for knowledge. Remember to seek Him first and let Him guide you to your abundant and eternal destination. The fear of the Lord is the beginning of wisdom. As you transform your life through Christ, ask yourself, "What are some of the most important things I need to know?"

Let's begin by asking this question, "What is my purpose?" Every child of God serves a purpose for the glory of God. Sometimes, it may seem odd and you may not understand. However, if you lack understanding, you should ask God as He will give liberally to those who ask. In your eyes, some things don't make sense. But remember, God knows what He is doing. He does not make mistakes.

The man who was born blind had a purpose. His blindness brought glory to the name of God.

God was glorified through this man's healing. Lazarus, who was a friend of Jesus, was sick to death. They called for Jesus to come and heal him, but Jesus chose not to come when they wanted Him. He came when it was time for His name to be manifested to the people, not just as a healer as they already knew Him as such, but also as the resurrection and the life.

You might get mad with God when you don't fully trust Him, and, in your limited understanding, you want things done your way and in your time. Lazarus' death also served a purpose. Some may reason and argue about this and ask what sense it makes. Well, it makes all the sense in the world because what God does is well done, even when you can't see the logic behind it. He is God and will always be God with or without you and me.

Maybe what you are going through is to bring glory to God's name. When you accept that nothing God does is a waste of time, you will learn to trust Him and know He is working out His purpose in you. I encourage you to hold on because God has not brought you this far to leave you. There is a cure for your hurt: Jesus. He is the only solution and the best friend you could ever have.

After all, what does this world have to offer you? You are just passing through. What shall it profit you to gain the whole world and lose your own soul? What shall you give in exchange for your soul? Nothing is worth the while.

The one person who can truly answer these questions is you. If you answer these questions wisely, it will lead you right back to the beginning of the original question: what is my purpose? The whole duty of man is to fear God and keep His commandments (Ecclesiastes 12:13). During difficult and challenging times, you may find it hard to fully trust Him. These are the most crucial times when you need divine strength to make it through your trials. There is a lesson to be learned in every trial you go through.

In the most painful times in your life, you are being groomed for effective ministry. You will come to understand that you can minister to others more effectively when they are going through pain because you have been there. What better teacher in the classroom of life than that of your own experience?

Can you see why you are encouraged to count it all joy when we fall into various trials (James 1:2-4)? Trials breed faith and faith breeds patience. Patience will become mature in you, making you complete, and nothing will be missing. This is the quality you need to truly say you possess the fruit of the Spirit.

Having the fruit of the Spirit and demonstrating it in times of tribulation is a good sign of maturity in your relationship with Christ and your fellow brothers and sisters. If you have faith and patience, you have learned how to wait on God.

Do you possess the fruit of the Spirit?

> *"But the fruit of the Spirit is love, joy, peace, longsuffering, gentleness, goodness, faith, Meekness, temperance:..."* (Galatians 5:22-23).

How much do you demonstrate the fruit when you are going through what is called the darkest times of your life? I know it is hard, and you will not accomplish this by yourself, but it can be done. The apostle Paul reminded us in the Book of Romans that we can do all things through Christ who strengthens us. When we are hurting and experiencing pain and challenges we do not understand, it is the time to stand still and see the salvation of our God. What can our God do? Prove what He can do for you. It doesn't matter how hard it is or how hard it becomes, you must pass this test or you will have to retake it.

If you fall short of any of the above, you must reexamine yourself to see what is taking place or what is missing. Seek help from God so His fruit will be manifested in your life at these crucial times.

This is how the fire proves your love for God. The apostle Paul asks a profound question: what shall separate me from the love of God? Take a minute and read Romans 8:38-39.

Let the Word of God correct your life. It was given by inspiration and is good for doctrine, correction, and reproof. Let God's Word become the light to guide your footsteps in the path He has chosen for you. Do not allow the dark and troublesome seasons of life to shake your faith in Christ.

What is God's Position for Your Life?

God's position is that you may have life abundantly. You may wonder why He uses the word "may." This suggests that He gives us free will, just as He gives us free gift.

"For God so loved the world, that he gave his only begotten Son, that whosoever believeth in him should not perish, but have everlasting life" (John 3:16).

The promise of everlasting life doesn't exempt you from trials in this life. Everlasting life is promised to those who have accepted Christ as Lord and Savior and endure to the end. If you have done so, you will spend eternity with God in a place without pain or sorrow, but the reality is once you are in this life, you will face tribulation.

Praise the Lord, God freely gave us the gift of eternal life and you must also freely receive it. Those who reject God's precious gift are doomed for eternity. Will you believe God right now? Will you make this confession right now?

> I believe Jesus is the Son of God and He came in the flesh and died for the remission of my sins. I accept the Lord Jesus as my personal Lord and Savior.

This kind of prayer and confession is accepted and will lead you into a personal relationship with Him. This now behooves you to obey His Words and bring you into your rights as a son or daughter. You're now a joint heir with Jesus and have rights to the tree of life.

You must change your lifestyle to be in harmony with God's Word because His Word will not change to accommodate your ways. Scripture says, "There is a way which seemeth right unto a man, but the end thereof are the ways of death" (Proverbs 14:12). Jesus told us He is the way, the truth, and the life. So, there can't be any significant life without Jesus Christ. The fear of the Lord is the beginning of wisdom (Proverbs 9:10).

Let wisdom have its perfect way in you. As said before, if any man lacks wisdom, let him ask of God who gives unto every man liberally, according to the measure of faith (James 1:5-8). Acknowledge God in all your ways and ask Him for guidance, direction, and clarity so you may please Him. When your ways are pleasing to Him, He will cause even your very enemies to be at peace with you (Proverbs 16:7). What great contentment and unmerited favor—praise be to God.

Let Us Pray

Dear Daddy Jesus, You live in me. I can do all things through Christ who strengthens me. I have this confidence only because of You, Lord. According to Your Word in Philippians 1:6, I know that You have started a good work in me and You will bring it to fruition until You come back. Bless Your Name, Jesus. I pray like the Apostle Paul in Ephesians 6:19-20 that I may open my mouth and speak boldly. Lord, fill me with

Your Words, inspiration, wisdom, knowledge, and understanding as I seek to represent You. Lord, grant me Your protection. Keep me from the evil of this world. I will not be afraid of what man can do unto me, but I will fear Your Name, O' Lord. You are my beginning and end, my first and last. You are the I AM. You are the Alpha, the Omega and You are my God in whom I trust. In Jesus' Name, Amen.

Remember, carefully choose those with whom you share your vision. Do not be deceived; many dream killers are out there.

I am aware that you have read this earlier in the book. Now, I am asking you to meditate on this.

A Crushed Dream

A dream I never got to wake up from

And lived like I always wanted to win.

I dream that I would one day reach the stars,

And like they say, the sky is the limit to what you can have.

I never knew the way to reach it because no one showed me how

And those who did the climb never left an ounce of its trace behind.

You couldn't follow their trail; the secret they did not unveil or reveal.

As I gazed into space, my life seemed to just go to waste

Never knowing that I too could be great.

If only I had the faith,

When all that's inside me lie await.

Just what I needed to be liberated,

I thought had drifted too far never to be
emancipated.

When I could have been way ahead,

Just as I often anticipated.

Never knew the light was so brightly shining

And many saw the warning

That one day, I would be liberated

To live the dreams I always wanted.

There is a door widely open to enter in

To be reinvented, educated, and rejuvenated

To stop reaching for the stars, just be one and
start shining right where you are.

You don't have to go that far

To make all the impressions.

Yet, you will need some aggression

To make the implication that will find the solution

And to tell the next generation the way to satisfaction is through salvation.

By Pastor Vendrix Headley

CHAPTER 7

Jesus is Our Peace

In the Scripture, God promises that when you keep your mind stayed on Him, you will not only have peace but perfect peace (Isaiah 26:3). He further announces a special blessing if you delight yourself in His law and meditate on them day and night (Psalm 1:2). These are favored verses that people often recite from their childhood days. I dare you to take a moment and meditate on these scriptures with me.

Let's understand the concept of meditation. Do not take it lightly, or you may not even want to read a scripture verse you already know. Meditation is biblical. God gave us the concept, but many of us do not utilize it. God calls you blessed when you meditate on His Words.

In simple terms, meditation is a way of digesting what you have read, giving you the opportunity to ponder or think about it. This leaves you in a state of awe.

The Shepherd's Psalm

Let's reason as we dissect this Psalm 23 together.

"The Lord is my shepherd; I shall not want. He makes me to lie down in green pasture; He leads me beside the still waters, He restores my soul; He leads me in the paths of righteousness For His name's sake. Yea, though I walk through the valley of the shadow of death, I will fear no evil; For You are with me; Your rod and Your staff, they comfort me. You prepare a table before me in the presence of my enemies; You anoint my head with oil; My cup runs over. Surely goodness and mercy shall follow me All the days of my life; And I will dwell in the house of the Lord Forever" (Psalm 23 NKJV).

You are Special

Did you notice the personal and complete relationship between the Good Shepherd (the Lord) and His sheep in this scripture? Pay attention. Notice that you are never alone, and this scripture was written with you in mind. Take note of how it was formulated:

The Lord is my…
I shall…
He makes me…

He leads me…
He restores my…
He leads me…
Yea, though I…
For You are with me…
Your rod and Your staff, they comfort me…
You prepare a table before me…
You anoint my head…
My cup runs over…
My life…
I will…

This scripture speaks strictly about the relationship between you and God. Notice the personal pronouns used: he, me, my, and I. Did you see any mention of anyone else appearing in this specially designed scripture? It is exclusively yours (you and the Shepherd).

There is another stunning revelation and underlying and profound truth here. Although I see you and the Shepherd only in this scripture, each individual is uniquely placed in a singular position. Everyone can fit into this "you and the Shepherd" position without interfering with the other person's relationship with the Shepherd. This is what makes each one who comes into this dynamic relationship with Jesus so special. This is a one-of-a-kind universal love that is individually complete for everyone who comes to Him.

What would you give in exchange for this kind of eternal protection and love? Your confidence should be built up just to know you are qualified through the blood of Jesus to experience such love as this.

Have you ever seen a love like this? There is none to be compared to this unconditional, undying love.

Take a moment to meditate on Psalm 23. Let your soul muse on the inseparable love of God. Can you feel the sweet spirit? Can you feel the love as you think about Him? Oh, what joy it brings to know that someone really and truly loves you.

Let these deep unfathomable thoughts pierce your mind and spirit. Let it be an eternal part of your life. And do not be lost in the wonders of it all.

Allow your thoughts and meditation to be lost in this wonderful, undying and unconditional one-of-a-kind love. The apostle Paul says, "Who shall separate us from the love of Christ? Shall tribulation, or distress, or persecution, or famine, or nakedness, or peril, or sword?" (Romans 8:35 NKJV). No! Nothing shall separate us from this inseparable love. Stay connected.

Let Us Pray

Thank You, God, for Your peace that surpasses all understanding, protection, covering, and Your love. O' Lord, You promised that if I keep my mind stayed on You, I will have everlasting peace. As I dwell in Your secret place, You will reveal mysteries to me. You promised peace even in the eyes of the storm. Father, only You can do the impossible. You show up right on time when my world turns upside down. O' God, You are great. You do miracles so great. There is no one else like You. I am confident of Your trust, faithfulness, grace, and mercy. Your grace has been sufficient. It is what has brought me safe thus far and it will lead me home. Thank You, Jesus.

CHAPTER 8

In Your Darkest Times

When you are faced with dark and dreadful times in your life, there is some consolation you can fall back on. Many times, we read the stories in the Word of God and we do not allow them to teach us valuable life lessons. We can emulate the godly characters in these stories in the Bible. These patriarchs were real people like you and me. Let's look at Joseph and what he went through. It is the worst thing when the enemy tries to hurt us, but it is even more devastating when our own flesh and blood are crud and heartless toward us. In times like these, only the grace of God will take us through.

In these times, you need light. This is the light the darkness cannot comprehend; the darkness will flee at the presence of this light. You need to trust and hope in it. This light is Jesus. Joseph knew who he was and whose he was. He didn't lose sight of the only help he knew, God. What does it mean to trust? Trust is a firm belief in the honesty, and reliability of someone. It is confidence and hope in someone. The position of trust is concrete, unmovable, and firm. Therefore, you must confidently put your trust in Christ.

When David was afraid, he trusted in the Lord. God promised that those who trust in Him will never be ashamed. He is the resurrection and the light. He is the Good Shepherd who gives His life for His sheep. Do you believe this? If you do, your faith should be built up. Your attitude will reflect a God-filled and purpose-driven life. God will give to you according to the measure of your faith. How much do you see yourself receiving from God right now? Are you experiencing the abundant life He promised you? If you are not, examine yourself. If you examine the Word of God, you will see He always does what He says He will do. Let God be true and every man a liar. He is our peace in the midst of the storm.

I pray as you look at the life of Joseph, you will learn to put all your confidence in God who cannot fail. In Genesis 50:20, he uttered_these words, "You meant it for evil against me, but God meant it for good." What a perspective of one who embraced the God of heaven and completely trusted Him. I encourage you when life serves you a lemon, through faith, learn to make lemonade. What am I saying? As you face the pain, heartache, and mistreatment of this life, only your full and total surrender to God will help you overcome. As God turns your circumstances around, you will see your different challenges, hindrances, and stumbling blocks become your steppingstones through the power of God.

Let Us Pray

Dear Lord, please give me a humble heart to receive this counsel You are giving to me. It is not necessarily a new revelation, but a strong reinforcement. I will accept this basic revelation through Your Word and through Your servant whom You have chosen to use. In Jesus' Name, Amen.

God is Your Coach

It took me a long time to understand what it really means that **all things** work together for good. How could this be? This question must be addressed. I finally paid attention to whom it speaks. It particularly refers to individuals with purpose, those who are called and love God. I can understand clearly why and how our **hurt** will bring glory to God. When you understand this fact, you will beg to know that you are very special. It means God is guiding your steps all the way.

To give you a clearer picture of God's presence in your life in times of hurt or joy, you must understand and trust Him as your coach. You must be coachable, learn to take and follow instructions, and do exactly what He says.

A coach is a vehicle that takes you from where you are to where you ought to be, one who has gone before you and has experienced the same situations and succeeded. You must get on board with this special coach and never get off. He will take you to your eternal destination.

The result is seen in Genesis 50:20. All evil set up against God's call is already canceled.

All things work together for good. If truth be told, it makes no sense to us. It is a deeper revelation of the human consumption. It cannot be comprehended in the flesh. That is why many get frustrated, depressed, confused, and even turn away from God. Even though you may not see, feel, or hear Him at times, He is right there with you. You must believe He is doing something bigger than human understanding. What He says is exactly what it is.

"God is not a man, that He should lie, Nor a son of man, that He should repent. Has He said, and will He

not do? Or has He spoken, and will He not make it good?" (Numbers 23:19 NKJV).

What is a divine enigmatic may be mysterious or unfathomable. However, it must be understood through spiritual understanding and with the guidance of the Holy Spirit. When you demonstrate the love of God and have His call on your life, it's no more you but God and His purpose.

Purpose is the reason why something is done or created or for which something exists. It is also an intended desire or result.

Do not forget that you are called for God's purpose. When it comes to hurt for the cause of Christ, your own desire and selfish motives will diminish and die. This depicts the assassination of the flesh. It is the **flesh** that adds more hurt to you and others.

Non-Compliance

One aspect you must pay attention to is being disobedient to God's instructions. Disobedience can equal obliteration as stated in chapter 3. Hurt comes in numerous ways and for various reasons. You must identify what is causing your hurt. Check to see if you are in God's will. Are you walking contrary to what He desires of you? Stop here and examine yourself. This may just be the solution for your pain and hurt.

It is safe to say that hurt and pain are inevitable. It is a unique part of the human dynamic because of sin. Nevertheless, you were not left without salvation. There is hope! You have help! Jesus is the ultimate solution guaranteed. He is your coach. He has modeled for you how to handle hurt and pain. Jesus showed that it was not easy as He suffered and experienced unfortunate situations in His time on the earth. He recognized He was here for a purpose. Although He felt the agony, He gave Himself to the purpose of His Father and fulfilled God's will, so you too can be saved.

We were told we would have trials in this world. Christ admonished us to be courageous because He has overcome (John 16:33). He placed us in a unique position when He was leaving. He gave us peace that is incomprehensible to the natural man (John 14:27).

You can have peace even during the tumult. Yes, you can. This peace passes all understanding. In these times in which we are living, the world is confused and filled with fear about what's next. People are living on the edge and operating without hope. However, those who know and call upon Jehovah, Yahweh, will experience peace and comfort, knowing their help and hope come from the Lord. Hallelujah! Amen.

Timothy encourages you to endure hardship as a good soldier (2 Timothy 2:3-5). He urges you not to give up or give in to trials. You must suffer tribulation here in your journey. But endurance will finally get you the price and bring you to your destination to live eternally with God.

"Speak ye comfortably to Jerusalem, and cry unto her, that her warfare is accomplished, that her iniquity is pardoned: for she hath received of the Lord's hand double for all her sins" (Isaiah 40:2).

Let Him Out to Let Him In

Let Him out, so He can come in! You may not be ready for what God can do in your life if you place limitations on Him. What will it take to let Him out so He can come into your world? For decades, He's been locked in a box and only expected to show up in the little things. When things seem too big, it's forgotten that big problems are God's specialties. God is bigger than your problems and thoughts and His ways are past finding out.

In Psalm 24, the Lord gives you the authority to command the gate that encloses you and holds you captive to disappear. Open your mouths and speak these words:

"Lift up your heads, O ye gates; and be ye lift up, ye everlasting doors; and the King of glory shall come in. Who is this King of glory? The Lord strong and mighty, the Lord mighty in battle. Lift up your heads, O ye gates; even lift them up, ye everlasting doors; and the King of glory shall come in. Who is this King of glory? The Lord of hosts, he is the King of glory. Selah"
(Psalm 24:7-10).

You have the power to break the chains that have held you captive for years. You may need to break some yokes and shake some folks. Don't let them wear you out. Redesign your environment. You must choose those with whom you want to be surrounded. Avoid negative and one-track-minded people.

Some folks are not going anywhere and they do not want you to go either. You don't need to fight with anyone. You just respectfully need to ask for an excuse. Know your purpose. Equip yourself and commit your ways to the Lord. Delight yourself in the Lord, and He will give you the desires of your heart.

Learn to shout victory with a closed mouth. There is a place in the world for everyone. Don't let the odds or the obstacles stop you. Use obstacles as steppingstones. God has a plan for your life. He knows the plans He has for you, plans for good and not for evil. He plans to prosper you and give you an expected end. (Jeremiah 29:11)

Let Us Pray

Dear God, how great You are, Lord. You are marvelous and plenteous in compassion. You are exalted far above all gods. Who can understand God's error? Lord, what shall I render for all Your benefits? Lord, I will say like the psalmist, I will take the cup of salvation. I will pay my vow in the congregation of Your people. Thank You for being my Shepherd. Thanks for leading me in Your green pasture, Lord. Even sometimes when I am unruly, Your staff would pull me back in safely. What a might God, Shephard, You are. Lord, You are my light when it gets so dark, lonely and frightening. Lord, You are always there. Lord, although I only see one set of footprints in the sand, I know that You have me in Your arms and You are carrying me. O' God, I am forever grateful to You. Glory to Your Name. Amen.

CHAPTER 9

Be Grateful and Give Thanks

Be grateful and give thanks. It could have been worse. Always remember that in whatever state you find yourself, someone is in a worse situation.

People tend to give much attention to the negative things in life. Count your blessings and you will soon realize it's not so bad after all. If you have life, that's enough to be thankful for. Think about it. Some people do not have life; they are dead, so they cannot think, far less complain. Also, many people who are alive cannot move around. Some are in hospitals and other places where their movements are limited. Train your mind to think positively even when situations seem to be bad.

Believe it or not, out of every bad situation, there is a good in disguise. As said before, what the devil meant for evil, God turned it around for your good. Knowing this fact, you can now laugh because you are confident that despite how bad it may seem, the Master of your life is a specialist. He specializes in the impossible. Can you recall someone who has tried to do bad things to you? How did it work out? Well, you see there is not much to really complain about; just give thanks.

Did you know that all things, yes, all things work together for your good if you love the Lord and if you are called to His purpose? This fact is hard to digest, but if you are patient, you will see the end result. You will see you were never alone in that situation you went through. God is working things out in your favor.

Gratitude helps you see your blessings are far greater than you are willing to admit. The Lord has brought you from a mighty long way. Hasn't He always come through for you?

Well, He is the same yesterday, today, and forever, so why worry when you can pray? The songwriter says, "There's a roof up above me, a good place to sleep; food on my table and shoes on my feet; You gave me Your love, Lord, and a fine family; thank You, Lord, for Your blessings on me." Say thank you and be reminded to lift up your eyes to the hills from whence comes your help. Can you safely say your help cometh from the Lord who made heaven and the earth?

As Bright as a Star

I am an ambassador; this is what you say.

God didn't make you a star, an ambassador
instead.

I am not from Mars.

I am not for war,

A shining star by far.

Well, an ambassador and that's by far

Stars were made to shine and brighten up the
skies.

Though they sometimes die,

There is always light in the skies.

Shine, little star, shine!

Your glaze can be seen from afar.

Yes, there are many other stars.

There are bright stars, big stars, and powerful
stars.

You must let your light shine bright,

That men may see your good works

And be led to glorify your Father in heaven.

You will fulfill your purpose

Without the intimidation of other lights,
tinning lamps, lanterns, and flashlights.

As a star, you will always be shining
as it was made to be.

It was designed to give light,

And it glows in the dark

To brighten the way of others.

So, never stop shining.

Be a star designed from glory

To shine as bright as it can be.

You may say no star

But an ambassador, instead by far.

By Pastor Vendrix Headley

Arise!

Webster's dictionary defines the word "arise" as "to get up as out of bed, coming to being, to rise or ascend." It was in some of the most crucial and desperate times that the word "arise" was used by the greatest and most powerful Man who ever walked the earth. Jesus Christ, the Savior of the world, moved from place to place, bringing hope to the hopeless and help to the helpless. He gives us the command to follow in His footsteps.

He brought love and comfort to the lonely and forgotten. He even brought back the dead to life. God is bigger than your problems, and the struggles you may be facing today are mere steppingstones to propel you to arise from that situation. There is hope! You must be willing to wake up, smell the coffee, and put your senses to work. Position yourself for your blessing. As it is said, "While there is life, there is hope," and that's a good place to begin.

You must be in a downward position to obey that powerful command, "Arise!" If you are feeling down and it seems there is no way out, your breakthrough is here. It's your time. It's your season, so take heed to this command and arise. Even if your situation is dead and now "stinketh," that is more reason to arise and look up.

The Resurrector is here. He is Jesus the life-giver, and He wants you to have abundant life. Be reminded there is no satisfaction without salvation.

Your success begins when you put first things first. Scripture encourages us to seek God and His righteousness first and all other things will be added unto us (Matthew 6:33). In the psalms, David witnessed God's faithfulness firsthand when he declared, "I have been young, and now am old; Yet I have not seen the righteous forsaken, Nor his descendants begging bread" (Psalm 37:25 NKJV).

Do some self-examination and "to thine own self be true." Don't live only on your own expectation. Trust God who is the almighty (all mighty). He will do the impossible for you. His ways are different from your ways. His thoughts are way higher than your thoughts, so with this truth, you can now see where you are today, why you are there, and do the next best thing—arise!

We have all found ourselves in positions where we wanted things done our way, and in our time; that, my friend, is a big problem because, in God's book, we are setting ourselves up for failure. Let me bring to your attention one of the most remarkable factual stories recorded in the Bible in

John Chapter 11. The story tells of Lazarus, Mary, and Martha who were very close friends of Jesus.

For several years, they knew Jesus as a faithful friend, a teacher, a comforter, and the greatest healer. Lazarus was very dear to Jesus. While Jesus was away on one of His journeys, Lazarus became sick. His sisters sent word to Jesus to come quickly because their beloved brother and His dear friend was gravely ill and needed Him there with them right away. They knew without a doubt that Jesus could do something for their sick brother.

At that time, Jesus may have felt the need to give a greater gift to His friends than merely healing sickness, so He did not show up. Consequently, their situation grew worse, and Lazarus died. Mary and Martha were so overcome with grief, they wept for their beloved brother.

This was a natural thing to do, and their neighbors and friends joined in the mourning as they sympathized with their situation, which was gruesome. Even though they looked for Jesus to come, there was no sign of Him, so the funeral took place. Four days passed and then came Jesus. If I were Mary and Martha, I would not have wanted to see Him then. Why did He wait until Lazarus died to turn up? No wonder some folks lose hope to the point of taking their own lives.

Jesus needed to reveal to His friends that He was much more than what they knew Him to be. He deliberately delayed His arrival to bring about the miracle they needed most. God's miraculous greatness is best realized when we have to exercise our faith beyond the natural realm.

Though disappointed at first, Martha ran out to meet Jesus when He showed up. However, Mary did not come out to offer that kind of greeting. Perhaps she was annoyed with the Master as some of us get at times when things do not go the way we want them. Martha said, "Lord, if you had been here, our brother would still be alive."

Time is insignificant with Jesus. A thousand years in our sight is but a day to Him. Jesus was moved with compassion because of His love, and He wept for His friend. He then asked to be shown the place where they buried Lazarus.

Martha told Jesus it was no use anymore because Lazarus had already been buried for four days and he was now beyond rotten and stunk. Not so fast, Martha! There is always hope when Jesus arrives on the scene. You can place your trust in Him.

Jesus' response to her was that it was not a problem because, "I am the resurrection and the life" (John 11:25).

Jesus then told them to roll away the stone. They obeyed amidst much apprehension of the stench that would follow. Jesus then prayed to His Father before everyone, and, with a loud voice He called out, "Lazarus, come forth!" And the impossible became possible. He who was dead and buried obeyed the voice of Jesus and arose from the dead.

My friend, many times the stones in your life become hindrances and block your blessings. But I encourage you to listen to the voice of our Lord. Roll the stones out of your way and watch God do for you what no other on the earth can do. Remember, God can do more for you in one minute than you can do for yourself in a lifetime. May God grant you the strength and courage to wake up and arise. In Jesus' name.

Let Us Pray

Lord, I rise to give You thanks for all You have done. Lord, I say if it had not been for the Lord on my side, where would I be. I give You thanks. There is so much going on around me, Lord. I am not lucky, am not better than anyone else yet You kept me. You protect me, my family and my friends. God, I am grateful. You remind me in Your Word to give thanks, for You are good and Your mercies endure forever. Thank You, Lord. Words are not enough to tell You thanks. O' Lord, my Lord, how majestic is Your Name in all the earth. You are God all by Yourself. I honor You. I praise You forever. In Jesus' Name, Amen.

CHAPTER 10

Let's Face Reality

If you are facing challenges today, you are not alone. You are not the first and you will not be the last. You may be surprised to know how many others are going through similar situations or worse.

The question is often asked: what do you do when you don't know what to do? It all comes down to one common thing: choice.

Whatever you choose to do when you are going through a particular situation will affect you in one way or another. Life is a journey with many different roads. Whichever you choose, it will lead you to a destination. It's not where you start but where you finish.

Your destiny is in your hand, and it's all a part of God's plan. There is always a solution, but you must be strong. You must take responsibility for your actions, and I guarantee you, it will bring satisfaction.

Many people are stuck in their beginnings. They are held captive by the arrows of their past and are unable to move forward or put their past behind them. They tend to blame others for their failures in life.

We are cognizant of the fact that our parents are responsible for molding us and preparing us for the future. Unfortunately, many of our parents were not educated and were unable to supply us with the correct tools we needed to move on successfully to the future.

Your parents had their roles to play up to a certain stage of your life. You are the biggest part of what you become in life. You must take responsibility for your actions.

Life can be very difficult, and you may find it really hard to break through to the turning point. However, with determination and ambitious goals, you will find a way to drive yourself in the correct gear. Therefore, you cannot blame anyone for who you are in life today. The choices you make will either make it better or worse for you.

Many others have been in worse situations than yours, and they were able to turn them around and make something worthwhile of themselves. It is not time for self-pity or patronizing; it's all in you. God has given everyone gifts according to their abilities. You may just need to be stirred up with that gift so you can see and use what's in your hand.

Let Us Pray

Dear Lord, I pray that You will give me the courage to face the reality of this life. O' God, there is nothing new under the sun. The patriarchs have gone through similar experiences, yet they did not give up. Lord, please help me to be strong and in the power of Your might. Help me to put on the whole armer of God so I will be able to stand in these days. Jesus, You are my greatest example. You have gone through many things for me. Now, it's my time to do the same. The fact that You had the power to call millions of Angels to stop You from going through all the evil You encountered, You did it anyway, knowing what it would have been and Lord, You did it for me. I will say like You did, it's not my will but thine be done. Grant me the courage in Jesus' Name I pray. Amen.

CHAPTER 11

To Be Pure

It's not an overnight thing. *"To the pure all things are pure…"* (Titus 1:15 NKJV). Purity qualifies you for the kingdom of God. If you ask who is pure, all hands would go up. But not so fast, mister! How did you become so pure? You were born in sin and shaped in iniquity. Have you identified the impurities in you? Have you confronted them?

If you did, you would recognize to remain pure, you must be God-conscious by the second. It is so easy to become impure; however, it is not impossible to be pure. With honesty, a conscious prayer life, a sincere desire to follow God, and with His help, you can be pure. Also, you must surrender to God to remain pure.

We are humans with a sinful nature, and we live in a world that is also sinful, so we are in a constant fight to stay pure. Being pure is having no trace of evil thoughts, harboring unsettled disputes that interfere with our inner peace, or any other thoughts that are not in total unity with what the Word of God teaches.

The mind plays a big part in the process of purity. It is a very powerful weapon; therefore, you should guard it well because sometimes, it can become unruly and uncontrollable. Taking control of the mind is one sure way to help cultivate purity. What you allow to remain in the mind is very important.

Two factors want to govern the mind: the flesh and the spirit. They are constantly at war with each other to rule the mind. This is a hard battle and cannot be won by your own might or power. The desire of the flesh is great and very powerful, but so is the spirit. Unfortunately, most of the time, the flesh gets the better of you. If you do not crucify the flesh and renew your mind constantly, you will never be pure.

How often do you have to remind yourself of who you are? You are so easily offended by words and even the ways of others around you, that you must make a conscious effort to bear the pain and not fulfill fleshly desires. This is not an easy task, but you can do all things through Christ who strengthens you. By God's grace and mercy, you can gain victory.

Knowing the great benefits and rewards to be gained from being pure, and that the kingdom of God awaits you, will motivate you to strive for purity. What greater gain is there than to know you are a part of God's eternal kingdom? Purity comes from being honest and having enough self-control to make the right choices.

Be Honest

Being honest means that you say what you mean and mean what you say. That is the way God does things. He honors His Word above His name. His Words will not return unto Him void but they will accomplish what He sends them to do (Isaiah 55:11).

Remember that God will not take it lightly if you do not value and weigh your words before you speak them. Words are powerful and can cause eternal scars. The impact can be devastating, especially on those who are weak and cannot combat those attacks.

Self-Control

Ask God for the will to have self-control in every area of your life. Do not be driven by your every emotion or your ego, knowing you have the potential to do the wrong thing. With discipline, determination, and making the right choices, you will ultimately choose to do the right thing when you are rubbed the wrong way. Let integrity instantly uphold you. Many times, people want to act on their pressing emotions, but they must be tempered by the Holy Spirit. He will restrain you and the peace of God that passes all understanding will take control of your actions and you will find that it will dictate those instants of displeasure.

I am Kinuna

In many instances, the accuser lurks around waiting on us to slip, so he can condemn and accuse us. Then he puts a stop sign in front of us. Sadly enough, we fall prey to his false authority. As a child of God, the enemy has nothing on you. You are privileged. You have an Advocate, our Mediator who has given us grace seven times seven. Dearly beloved, know your kingdom rights. Scripture says that a righteous man falls seven times and rises seven times (Proverbs 24:16).

Don't stay condemned by anyone or anything when your Savior has given what is called Kinuna, which means newness. God's indomitable power is seen in 2 Corinthians 5:17-21 giving us total victory over every other power. He told us our own hearts are not great enough to condemn us, so where would the accuser stand?

I stand to encourage you to demonstrate Kinuna. Looking at 2 Corinthians 5:17, you will see you can experience a spiritual rebirth, a regeneration of your spiritual being. It means you are a new creation. The old Adamic nature dies, and you no longer live after the flesh but after the Spirit.

You are admonished to be transformed; this can only be obtained by renewing your mind daily. If you live in this daily renewal, then yesterday's mistakes or failures have no power over you and you are free from the bondage of the past. The enemy is always seeking to bring back your past because his job is to stop the completion of the work God has assigned you.

As a new creature, only unadulterated milk will help you to grow from strength to strength, and in grace and courage. Then you will be strong enough to eat solid food that matures your faith. Hence, you move on to maintaining your new life in Christ as you fix your mind on Him. You will experience perfect peace.

Engulf your mind with life-giving thoughts as recorded in Philippians 4:8. Think on things that are valuable and virtuous. Think on what is truthful, honest, just, pure, lovely, worthy of praise, and of good report. In doing so, you will plant yourself by the streams of living, fresh water. You will bloom. Your fruit will come forth in its season and God will be glorified in your life.

A Crushed Dream

A dream I never got to wake up from

And lived like I always wanted to win.

I dream that I would one day reach the stars,

And like they say, the sky is the limit to what
you can have.

I never knew the way to reach it because no one
showed me how

And those who did the climb never left an
ounce of its trace behind.

You couldn't follow their trail; the secret they
did not unveil or reveal.

As I gazed into space, my life seemed to just go
to waste

Never knowing that I too could be great.

If only I had the faith,

When all that's inside me lie await.

Just what I needed to be liberated,

I thought had drifted too far never to be
emancipated.

When I could have been way ahead,

Just as I often anticipated.

Never knew the light was so brightly shining

And many saw the warning

That one day, I would be liberated

To live the dreams I always wanted.

There is a door widely open to enter in

To be reinvented, educated, and rejuvenated

To stop reaching for the stars, just be one and
start shining right where you are.

You don't have to go that far

To make all the impressions.

Yet, you will need some aggression

To make the implication that will find the
solution

And to tell the next generation the way to satisfaction is through salvation.

By Pastor Vendrix Headley

Love Is Beautiful

Love is beautiful

Love is kind

Love is passionate

And so are you

Each time your eyes look into mine

You ignite the fire I cannot hide

My heart glows

My joy flows

And that's how I know

That love like yours is one of a kind

By Pastor Vendrix Headley

The Hidden Immeasurable Treasure

Take away the clock and you will see the joke

Under which lies precious treasurers, acres of
diamonds, and pearls,

Encumbered with the world: envy, jealousy,
malice, and strife

Break the yoke, and let wealth spring forth

Under which lies fresh flowing streams,
fountains of pure living waters

Drink to your health; take for your wealth

Do it for yourself

Let the stream break forth

By Pastor Vendrix Headley

You are the Watered Garden of God

A watered garden of God planted by the rivers of water that bringeth forth fruit in its season. Its leaf shall not wither and whatsoever he doeth shall prosper (Job 42:3). Your cup shall be full and running over. Goodness and mercy shall follow you all the days of your life (Psalm 23:6). Continue to dwell in God's presence forever.

Let Us Pray

Lord, who shall ascend into the hill of the Lord? Or who shall stand in thy Holy place? In Psalm 24:3-6, Your Word declares that he who has a clean hand and a pure heart, who have not lift up their soul unto vanity, nor sworn deceitfully shall receive the blessing of the Lord, and righteousness from the God of our Salvation. Father, search me, O' Lord, and know my heart. I pray, Lord, that if there be some wicked ways in me, You will cleanse me from every sin and set me free. I will meditate on Your Words day and night. You pronounce a blessing for those who carry Your Words in their heart. David states, thy word have I hid in my heart that I might not sin against thee. Lord, You give me the remedy in Philippians 4:8 that I should think on good things that will keep me pure and clean. Whatsoever things are true, honest, just, pure, lovely, and are of good report, these are what keep me focused. Bless the Lord. Amen.

CHAPTER 12

It's Amazing What Praise Can Do

Praise is giving adoration to people for something they do. It is that which tells others how wonderful they are and the remarkable works they have done. Understand that praise involves at least a two-way exchange.

Both parties will benefit from this act, which is called praise. Usually, praise is offered when an outstanding and extraordinary thing is being done; it can make a big difference in one's life, both to the giver and the receiver.

The giver will be encouraged to continue to do marvelous things, and the receiver would have played their part in encouraging someone to keep doing well.

Praise motivates people to do good deeds. Something extraordinary happens and a relationship with trust and confidence grows between those two individuals.

God is the One most worthy of all praise. Praises belong to Him. Everything that has breath should engage in this awesome and wonderful exercise. The more you praise God, the more blessings He bestows upon you. Praise is a powerful tool you must use, even in your lowest times when you don't feel like doing it. Praise confuses the enemy and brings healing to your soul.

Our God loves praises so much that He lives in them. He inhabits our praises. He wants us to praise Him, so He will give us a song, even when everything seems to be going wrong.

When you begin to offer praises to God, your darkness will turn to day, and your heavy burdens become light. Your spirit is alive and you want to live. Delight yourself in God and He will give you the desires of your heart. If you need victory over anything, just begin to praise God. The children of Israel used praise as a weapon against their enemies and God gave them victory.

When Hezekiah was told he was going to die, he turned to the wall and worshiped God, and he lived for fifteen years more. Job worshiped God when He was going through the dilemma of his life to the point where he lost everything, including his children, and he was restored triple fold. Praise is a powerful tool you have in your hands. Use it and turn your situation around.

Worship is the Heart of God

We all want to get to the hearts of the ones we love. Knowing how and finding the secret is the key. Let me hasten to tell you that the secret to the heart of God is worship. Since worship is the heart of God, you should endeavor to possess His heart. Your life must always reflect God through worship. Every activity you are engaged in, and every decision you make must bring glory to God.

Your daily life must be of worship. One person puts it this way, "Worship is life and life is worship." If you can digest and cherish this fact in your mind and spirit, you will become a living worshiper. The things you do in your daily walk are acts of worship but you can reach deeper when you carry out the solemn aspect of worship called adoration. This is when the flesh disappears, and the spirit is entwined with God's Spirit. Worship erupts from our souls to His. As you adore God, He draws you into His glorious splendor, and you fall into ecstasy. The expressions of your heart breathes out groanings that cannot be uttered. You cannot miss the fact that when in His presence, the awesome majestic splendor that enfolds you brings you to a place of awe.

Great and marvelous experiences will take place only when self and human desire diminish. The transformation of flesh into spirit takes place, and you will experience that divine encounter with your Creator. This is the place where you can truly commune as a friend to a friend.

The psalmist says deep calleth unto deep at the noise of the water sprout. This is the kind of worship that God desires from anyone who seeks to worship Him. This is the highest expression any human can ever experience.

God has a standard of how He wants to be worshiped, and anything that falls below His standard is unacceptable to Him. God told us that He is a spirit and when we worship, it can only be done in spirit and truth. This is the only time true worship takes place. Note as you get closer to the reality of worship, you will begin to understand it really begins when you enter the inner courts of God, which I will talk about in-depth in my next book, *From Hurt to Glory*.

God beseeches us that when we worship Him, we must do it in spirit and truth because He is a spirit. This suggests that He wants you to connect to that which is beyond the flesh. Every child of

God possesses a spirit. You must actively seek to understand what it means to worship God "in spirit." The reality is the flesh is also a hindrance, which always fights against the spirit. If you are not vigilant, you can live in the flesh and fool yourself that it is otherwise. When your life is overtaken by the spirit, it will be obvious because everything about you will change. Your attitude toward God and the things of God will be different, and your life will reflect the holiness of God. We are reminded to be holy because God is holy.

Holiness connects you to this wonderful and glorious, divine encounter. No wonder the enemy tries to counterfeit this experience by astral projecting. Astral projecting is an experience in the demonic world where out-of-body experiences occur. This can in no way be compared to what you experience when you are lost in the wonders of worship to God.

Worship belongs to Jehovah God alone; therefore, you must worship God alone. This kind of majestic exercise cannot and should not be given to anything or anyone but God. He clearly states He will not share His glory with another (Isaiah 42:8).

Worship brings intimacy with God and man.

This is a heart-to-heart connection with the holy Jehovah. When you enter this realm of worship with God, there is no telling what can happen. This is a place where all impossibilities become possible through God.

This is where the glory of God will unfold and His majestic glory will captivate your entire being. It is a place of purity, and no human can enter without the ushering in of the Holy Spirit. This place of worship is not a place where sacrifices are offered. It is totally holy and sacred. This is not a place of atonement, for it's not where forgiveness is sought. This place is called the Holy of Holies. Before the Holy Spirit ushers you in, you would have already shed all unrighteousness at the outer courts.

The darkest thing becomes the brightest, and you share in the one and only incomparable experience of your lifetime. The songwriter rightly puts it this way, "In His presence there is fullness of joy and at His right hands there are pleasures for ever more. Oh, what fellowship divine to know I am His, and He is mine, in the presence of the Lord there is fullness of joy."

Not only is there fullness of joy but there are also everlasting pleasures and confidence. God reveals His secrets to us. Our eyes are open, and we see the great and awesome wonders of God. We stand in awe and cry out like the prophet Isaiah said, "Woe is me." The expressions coming from our lips will be glory, majesty, Master, and Counselor.

Even though the Holy of Holies is an awesome place, it can also become a dreadful place. The priests entered once per year into this awesome yet dreadful place. The mighty glory of God is a consuming fire, but God is almighty and He quenches fire. He is in control of His fire, so do not be afraid. Only fear God. Moses experienced the fire of God in the burning bush; yet, the bush was not consumed, nor was Moses. The children of Israel experienced the fire of God, but it did not consume them. The fire of God was not meant to consume His people, but to give light, protection, transformation, purification, and holiness.

Let Us Pray

Lord, I lift Your name on high. I love to sing You praises, O' God. Early in the morning, my songs shall rise to the Father. You inhabit my praise. Lord, You ask for a certain kind of worship; a worship that's true and from the heart. Lord, I give You my heart. I give You my soul. I live for You alone, O' God. Every step that I make, O'

Lord, have Your way in me. I love You, Lord. I lift my hands to praise You. I give You the glory, Lord. I praise You because You are highly exalted. All praise and glory belong to You, Lord. You are eternally worthy, Lord. In Jesus' Name, Amen.

Conclusion

The infallible solution for hurting people is Jesus Christ because true healing and complete satisfaction can only be found in Him. Jesus is the perfectly guaranteed remedy for the hurts we encounter on the journey to our destiny. Life is saturated with a multiplicity of challenges, but the solutions are to be found in the sacred Word of God, which contains the truths to navigate the course of our lives. As a matter of fact, Jesus Christ is the personification of truth, so ultimately, knowing Him is how we complete our journey successfully.

You must remember that early in this book we declared two very significant facts: one, there is a life-giver, and the other, there is a life-stealer. Based on your choice of the life-giver, Jesus Christ, you are certain to be aware of your privileged status as a son or daughter of the Creator and Savior. The life-stealer, though, tags along to steal, destroy, and abort your journey with God. Be mindful, however, that the calamities of life will occur intermittently because the life-stealer does not sleep, but Christ has already defeated him, and he cannot overpower you if you drench yourself in the knowledge of God's Word of truth. Every promise of God is a certified check on the bank of heaven and will never bounce for lack of sufficient funds. Have faith in God and cash the checks of His promises as you grapple with the challenges and adversities along life's journey.

In God's Word, you will find life, hope, comfort, solutions to life's problems, and the guarantee of overall victory in Jesus Christ your blessed Redeemer. You will learn to utilize spiritual tools such as faith, effective prayers, meditation, and devotion as you overcome the challenges of your journey. You will stand in peaceful stillness and witness the salvation of the Lord.

Remember also that Christ is the solid Rock of Ages upon which you stand, and you can build no other powerful foundation but upon Him. Such a foundation is unshakable, and the boisterous and raging storms of life cannot prevail against it. Jesus is your peace, so don't be afraid when walking through "the valley of the shadow of death." Contemplate the assurances of Psalm 23, and be brave as the Lord, the Good Shepherd, leads you through the difficulties in the valley.

Scripture reminds you to count it all joy when you face diverse temptations. You are special and the Lord wants to count on you, so He allows you to be tested above measure. Do you remember how the Lord boasted about Job? With confidence, He gave Satan authorization to touch Job. God knew Job and Job knew Him. You and I have not gone through anything like what Job endured. Yet, Job loved God and worshiped him the more.

Does the Lord know you? Do you know the Lord? Are you the person God can depend on to bring out His glory? Can He manifest Himself to mankind through you? Are you willing to be used as a Guinea pig of righteousness unto salvation? What if God has chosen you? Are you the best fit for Him?

When you go through dreadful times, you may sometimes wonder like David in the Book of Psalms why you are suffering while the wicked prosper. And like him, you may "almost slip" because you believe you should be the one succeeding. You like to see yourself as righteous and the doer of good deeds. You do all the right things, obey all His commandments, and wonder why bad things happen to good people. However, it is not about good or bad; it's about when God look down for the fittest person, He saw you. When He wants to bring glory to His name, He will use what He know best and not a stranger. The only time He will use a stranger is when you and I refuse to go through what seems to be the worst things in life, then He will raise up stones in our place.

The key to success is to always know there are lessons to be learned in everything you go through, even when it seems foolish and senseless. If you are convinced that all things—and I mean all things—work together for the good of those who love the Lord and are called to His purpose, the mystery is solved and your hurt will fade away. At the end of it all, you can truly say what the devil meant for evil, God has turned it around for your good.

Be on the lookout for the next book, *From Hurt to Glory,* which is part two of *God's Hurting People.*

About the Author

Pastor Vendrix Headley is a dedicated servant of God who serves the Lord with a passion. She is a loving wife and mother of two sons, Aniel and Nashon Headley.

The eighth of nine children, Vendrix was born to Mr. Remises Walker and Miss Daphne Butler in Jamaica, West Indies, in the cool, hilly interior of a small village in Albion Mountain in the parish of Saint Mary. She was called to be an evangelist at the very early age of eight when she had an encounter with God but was too young to understand the meaning of that special visitation. She experienced a meltdown of her heart with a particular empathy for people. This endowment overwhelmed her entire being as she wept sorrowfully before God exclaiming, "I am sorry for the people." When asked by her friend, "What people?" Vendrix replied, "I don't know." Though strange an experience, she later realized that God was endowing her with a passion for souls.

Vendrix willingly carries out the command of her Lord as recorded in Matthew 28:19-20, "Go therefore and make disciples of all the nations...teaching them to observe all things that I have commanded you; and lo, I am with you always, even to the end of the age." She has operated under the evangelistic calling for many years and is now an ordained pastor, preaching in local churches and internationally.

Vendrix received a Bachelor of Arts in Communication from the College of New Resource. She is a gifted, inspiring songwriter and a recording gospel minister who has written many unpublished inspirational poems and other works for different occasions. Her love for communication and public speaking piqued her interest in radio broadcasting, and she has been the host of the Dynamic Gospel Trail Program for over eighteen years. She also gives credit to Nichol Gordon for her first co-hosting assignment on "Life Sat Radio."

Vendrix's diversity of gifts and multifaceted talents brought out the entrepreneurial spirit in her. With a strong desire to further her education, she went to Kingston, the capital city of Jamaica, and attended the Excelsior Community College where she pursued a course in fashion designing.

She graduated and was also awarded a diploma of competency. During this time, it was a great struggle as she had little or no help to survive. However, she was determined to make something worthwhile of her life. While working with a small manufacturing company called Jog Tog in Spanish Town, she stayed with an Adventist family, the Scarlets. Thank God for their good hearts and the open doors. Eventually, she had to return to her hometown where everyone embraced her and, of course, was happy to have her back.

She began demonstrating her fashion designing skills from home but soon became discouraged because she was sewing and not being paid. She later moved into the town of Port Maria where she joined a wonderful friend who blessed her with space in a place she had already occupied. Things started getting better, and she employed three female assistants. Not long after, she got married and migrated to the USA.

Now, Vendrix is the CEO of her company, V-Nash-A-Nil Exclusive, with her own line of clothing and perfume. The love she has for encouraging others flows naturally from her heart. She is now persuaded that God is directing her into the area of Christian counseling and teaching others how to trust God in the darkest and most difficult times of their lives. She also counsels and teaches how to secure peace in the midst of a storm, while embracing your God-given gifts to live more abundant lives that can only be found in God.

Vendrix is in the process of launching her first gospel magazine titled, "Aryse," and you are also reading her first published book.

She gives God the credit for all her accolades. God has been good to her. She can't complain. Thanks to the Most High God for all He has done.

God's Hurting People Accountability Journal

WHAT DID I LEARN?

_____

_____

_____

_____

_____

PSALM 56:3

WHAT DO I NEED TO CHANGE?

_____

_____

_____

_____

_____

PSALM 51:10-12

WHAT TRUTH DO I NEED?

_____

_____

_____

_____

_____

_____

JOHN 14:6

I AM A PROMISE

_____

_____

_____

_____

_____

_____

JEREMIAH 29:11

I WILL MAKE IT BY TRUSTING
GOD'S WORDS

_____

_____

_____

_____

_____

_____

PROVERBS 3:5

MY COMMITMENTS

_____

_____

_____

_____

_____

_____

ROMANS 14:8

KNOWLEDGE:
A PREREQUISITE TO BE USED BY GOD

_____

_____

_____

_____

_____

_____

HOSEA 4:6

ALL THINGS ARE WORKING
TOGETHER FOR MY GOOD

_____

_____

_____

_____

_____

_____

ROMANS 8:28

WHEN I AM IN THE VALLEY

_____

_____

_____

_____

_____

_____

PSALM 23:4

WHO AM I?

_____

_____

_____

_____

_____

_____

PSALM 100

DON'T MISS MY DESTINY

_____

_____

_____

_____

_____

_____

JOHN 14:3

I AM SPECIAL
WHAT DID GOD SAY ABOUT ME?

_____

_____

_____

_____

_____

_____

1 PETER 2:29

GOD'S WORDS

_____

_____

_____

_____

_____

PSALM 138:2

LIFE AND DEATH ARE IN THE POWER OF THE TONGUE

_____

_____

_____

_____

_____

PROVERBS 18:21

TWO FACTS

_____

_____

_____

_____

_____

_____

JOHN 10:10

CONFIDENCE IN GOD

_____

_____

_____

_____

_____

_____

PSALM 123:1-2

WAITING ON GOD'S TIMING

_____

_____

_____

_____

_____

_____

ISAIAH 40:31

PEACE IN THE MIDST OF THE STORM

_____

_____

_____

_____

_____

ISAIAH 26:3

DON'T GIVE UP
GOD HAS A PLAN FOR ME

_____

_____

_____

_____

_____

_____

JEREMIAH 29:11

MY JOURNEY TO MY VICTORY

_____

_____

_____

_____

_____

_____

ROMANS 8:18

TAKE IT PERSONAL
GOD IS COUNTING ON ME

_____

_____

_____

_____

_____

JAMES 1:12

MY PAIN

_____

_____

_____

_____

_____

2 TIMOTHY 2:12

MY FEAR

_____

_____

_____

_____

_____

_____

REVELATION 12:4

WHEN ALONE, GOD NEEDS MY ATTENTION

_____

_____

_____

_____

_____

_____

PSALM 27:10

ADD MY PRAYERS

_____

_____

_____

_____

_____

_____

ROMANS 5:3-5
JAMES 5:16

ADD MY SCRIPTURES

_____

_____

_____

_____

_____

_____

2 TIMOTHY 2:15

ADD MY BIBLE VERSES

_____

_____

_____

_____

_____

_____

DECLARE THAT SPECIAL WORD OVER MY LIFE

_____

_____

_____

_____

_____

ISAIAH 54:17

I AM NOT ON PUNISHMENT
I AM CHOSEN

_____

_____

_____

_____

_____

_____

HEBREWS 12:6

I WILL BLESS GOD AT ALL TIMES

_____

_____

_____

_____

_____

_____

1 THESSALONIANS 5:16-18

I WANT TO HEAR WELL DONE

_____

_____

_____

_____

_____

_____

MATTHEW 25:21

IT WILL BE WORTH IT ALL

_____

_____

_____

_____

_____

_____

ROMANS 8:18

www.ingramcontent.com/pod-product-compliance
Lightning Source LLC
Chambersburg PA
CBHW060539130626
46553CB00002B/826